PICTURES OF BUDDHIST CEYLON AND OTHER PAPERS

PICTURES OF BUDDHIST CEYLON AND OTHER PAPERS

F. L. WOODWARD

GYAN

Published by

GYAN

Gyan Publishing House
5, Ansari Road
Daryaganj, New Delhi-110002
Phone: 011-47034999, 9811692060
E-mail: books@gyanbooks.com

Distribution Network
gyanbooks.com
India, USA, Canada, UK, Australia, France

ISBN : 978-81-212-3893-9 (PB)
First Published, Madras, 1914

2nd Impression 2020

Printed at: Gyan Press, Delhi.

Pictures of Buddhist Ceylon and Other Papers
Author: F. L. Woodward

PICTURES OF BUDDHIST CEYLON

AND OTHER PAPERS

BY

F. L. WOODWARD, M.A. (Cantab.), F.T.S.

Member of The Pali Text Society,

Principal of Mahinda Buddhist College,

Galle, Ceylon

THEOSOPHICAL PUBLISHING HOUSE

Adyar, Madras, India

1914

A Buḍḍha-Rupa.

To

SIRIUS

A LOVER OF CEYLON

For permission to translate apply to

THEOSOPHICAL PUBLISHING HOUSE

Adyar, Madras, India

CONTENTS

ILLUSTRATIONS

A BUḌḌHIST SABBATH IN CEYLON

THE light is breaking in the east. Already in the gloom of the tall trees the squirrel's strange chirping bark is heard, and the hoarse grating cough of the monkey mingles with the coppersmith's metallic note and the "earliest pipe of half-awakened bird". Dawn is at hand. Already *kā-kā*, the black crow, is impudently demanding his early meal. Yet a few moments and the sun will strike the brass pinnacle of the temple, and we must offer flowers as he rises, so let us hasten onwards.

It is a Buḍḍhist holy day, New Moon or Full Moon in the dry season, or maybe Wesak Day, the day of days, in Laṅka-Ḍīpa, the land beloved of the children of the Lord, the fairest isle on earth, where the yellow robe still studs the palm-groves, and the white dome of the *dāgaba* gleams beyond the nameless blue-green of the tracts of paddy-fields. So we bathe and don the simple garb of the *upāsaka*—lay-devotee—a vest and two white cloths, upper and lower. Thus clad, bare head and foot, like Roman senators in city garb, we join the little groups silently making their way to the temple on the hill. At the foot of the long stone stairs leading to the sacred place are women and children, also clad in white, bearing flat baskets of flowers, the fragrant *namal*, arlia and white jasmine, or lotus, pink and blue and white, blood-red hibiscus and golden sunflowers, and the huge sheath of areca blossom. Here, too, is a small band of youths, white-robed, about to take with us the eightfold vows or *aṭṭha-sīla* for the first time in this life. There is just a touch of chill in the air, and some have drawn their upper robe over the head, and at a distance look like hooded nuns. This is for them a solemn day, marking the desire to be also of those who have set their faces towards the stream, a mark of admission to the outer court of the true community of Buḍḍha-puṭṭā, sons of the Buḍḍha.

On this holy day, when especial influences are shed upon the earth, especial merit may be gained by those who keep the eight vows, the layman's five of every day, and the extra three and perfected third precept kept by those who wish to take a further step. By taking the full ten vows one is, as it were, an ordained monk or *bhikkhu*. For said the Buḍḍha.

> He who would be like me should truly keep
> The eight vows on the eighth and fourteenth day
> And fifteenth of the half-month of the moon,
> As well as in the monk's retreat.[1]

For beneath the shadow of such an one, living the righteous life, as beneath the shadow of a mighty tree,

[1] *Anguttara-Nikāya*, iii, 37.

his wife and children, relatives and friends and all dependent on him will assuredly prosper. Thus, again, in a stanza are set forth the duties of the day:

He who has taken all the Precepts Eight
Kills not, nor steals, nor speaketh words untrue,
Nor dulls the brain with drugs, and from all deeds
Of lust abstains; nor does he eat at night
Or at forbidden seasons; nor with flowers
Adorn his body, nor use scents, but sleeps
On a mat spread on the ground. This is the Fast
With the observance of the Precepts Eight.
Thus by the Buḍḍha, the Enlightened One,
Who hath all sorrow ended, as the Path
To end all sorrow, this hath been declared.[1]

"*Puññāni katvāna,* (by working merit)," say the stanzas, "great fruits are gained for this life and the lives to come, whether in this world, or in other worlds unborn." And it is by this acceptance of the Ḍhamma, the Law of Life, by working in harmony with it, that the Buḍḍhist hopes to attain the perfect harmony, one touch of which will liberate him for ever from the ceaselessly-revolving wheel of *samsara,* existence. All the wealth of oriental imagery is employed to add lustre to the merit thus acquired. Listen again to the Buḍḍha's words:

The sun and moon, the sight of which is sweet,
Move to and fro, and in fixed bounds give light,
Dispelling gloom and shining in the skies.
Within this Cakkavāla[2] there are pearls,

[1] *Aṅguttara-Nikāya,* iii, 70.
[2] World-system.

Gems, cat's-eyes, Singi gold, Kancana[1] gold,
Kātaka and Jāta gold—yet all of these
One quarter of a quarter are not worth
Of merit gained, resulting from the Fast
With the observance of the Precepts Eight;
Just as the light of multitudes of stars
One quarter of a quarter is not worth
Of all the light shed by the moon alone.
Therefore the man of virtue and the woman
Who keep the Fast and keep the Precepts Eight,
Performing merit fruitful of results,
In the heaven-world are born without reproach.

While such thoughts as these have been passing through our mind, we have already climbed the long flight of steps and reach the sand-strewn court whose central figure is the skyward-tapering *dāgaba*, the dome-shaped relic shrine, whose blue-white graceful cupola pierces the dark green of the surrounding jak trees, and the sacred bo-tree, where already the squirrels are busy at their morning meal. Here, awaiting the coming of the officiating monk, stand in little groups some fifty men and women, white-robed and silent, each carrying on his arm a white cloth or towel, which will be used to spread upon the sandy ground during the act of worship. A subdued but joyous crowd. Glancing over the faces, one finds no trace of that pessimistic resignation which the ignorant always attribute to the followers of the Buḍḍha. Sorrow there may be in the world. True, this is the note of all religions; but to meet it with joyful hearts, with confidence of ultimate success, because the lives

[1] World-system.

Yatagala Rock Temple, Galle

are many, to be as merry as one may, that is the key-note of the Buḍḍhist life. Here is not ignorant idolatry, but devotion to One who has attained; and on this day we mean to tune up the strings of our whole being, if only for this single day, and we purpose to be Buḍḍha-puṭṭā, sons of the Buḍḍha, and like unto Him and His perfected monks. That is enough, not to fail or come short for this brief space, from now till to-morrow's dawn; this brings peace for the now, and merit, we think, which shall support our footsteps in troublous times, and lead us along the Path of Him who hath thus come and gone, *Ṭaṭhāgaṭo*, to the lotus-feet of the Lord Meṭṭeyya, who is yet to come.

First we must take *sīla*. This means asking the monk, who has just come out of his *vihāra*, or dwelling in the temple-court, to say for us the Pāli ritual, which we repeat after him, phrase by phrase. We gather round the big *dāgaba* or relic-chamber, against which stands the monk, facing outwards; spread our cloths and kneel, thrice bowing with the fivefold prostration of head and folded hands, body, knees and feet. There is a moment's silence. Then all repeat the triple invocation, words of power, the *namaskāra* to the Buḍḍha:

> Glory to Him, the Blessed Saint, the All-enlightened One.

Now the clear tones of the monk sound forth the *Tisaranaṁ*, the Threefold Refuge, which is repeated by the prostrate throng.

To the Buḍḍha for refuge I go.
To the Law for refuge I go.
To the Brotherhood for refuge I go.

This three times. Then follow the vows, repeated as before alternately.

From killing to abstain—the vow I take.
From stealing to abstain—the vow I take.
From lustful deeds to abstain—the vow I take.
From lying to abstain—the vow I take.
From drink and sloth-producing drugs to abstain—the vow I take.
From food at times unseasonable to abstain—the vow I take.
From dancing, singing, music, worldly shows,
From flowers, scents and unguents, and from wearing
Adornments and from beautifying this body,
From all these to abstain—the vow I take.
From couches high and broad to abstain—the vow I take.

Then follows silence. The devotees remain prostrate, meditating on the vows and repeating in a low voice certain stanzas composed by the Buḍḍha Himself, in praise of the Triple Gem—the Master, the Teaching, the Brethren—commencing: "*Iṭi pi so Bhagavā, Sammāsambuḍḍho.*" After some moments, one by one we rise and turn to the huge stone slab, now a mass of flowers. We fill our hands with these, first holding them out while a brother pours water, first on them, then on the flowers. Then with folded palms containing the flowers we offer some at each of the four little shrines surrounding the *dāgaba*, walking clockwise, till the circuit is complete. Then to the *Buḍḍha-ge* or image-house, where the huge stone *Rūpa* sits cross-legged in the silence, with downcast meditative eyes and lips of compassion. A flower or two yet remains, and these we offer to the bo-tree, in honour of the sacred tree sitting under which the Lord attained enlightenment. And now that we have retired, other relays of aspirants are arriving, and the same ceremony is gone through, and continues at intervals throughout the early morning.

It is now past six o'clock, and we proceed to the great hall close by, where the early morning meal is served to the devotees, who, for this one day, be it remembered, are as *bhikkhus* and are venerated by the other laymen who have taken only the five ordinary vows, and by them waited on with great respect. Mats and cushions are spread all along three sides of the hall, and the preaching platform occupies the upper end. Here we sit while the attendants bring us cups of tea or coffee, rice-cakes and plantains. This done we sit cross-legged upon the floor and meditate upon the vows and duties of the day, or on the Ḍhamma; no thought of business or the outside world should intrude. Some chant stanzas quietly, others read the sacred books, and this goes on till perhaps eight o'clock, when a monk arrives and silently takes his place upon the preaching chair. He delivers us a sermon on the merits to be acquired by this day's devotion. This is done in the Sinhalese tongue, the points of doctrine being driven home by quotations from the Pāli canon. From time to time a layman puts a question on some knotty point, to which the monk replies by quoting the Buḍḍha's words. There is no speculation. The canon is final. It is enough. You must not venture to add your *diṭṭhi* (view), to swell the sacred texts. It is this intense conservatism that has kept the Pāli text so well these two thousand years: but it must be admitted that often a solver of the knot is to be desired. No mere quotation of authority will satisfy this age of swelling knowledge, and very aptly does Mrs. C. Rhys Davids, one of the ablest of our western Buḍḍhist scholars, remark:

> And when we watch the way in which Goṭama Buḍḍha and his followers met the errors and the problems of their own day, recasting, it may be, a yet more ancient body of doctrine to cope with present needs, can we doubt that, if a Meṭṭeyya Buḍḍha arose here and now, he would recast their Ḍhamma, and, instead of making "converts" to a Norm adapted to bygone conditions, would evolve, with travail of soul, a gospel and a philosophy built out of the knowledge and the needs of to-day?[1]

So may it be.

This preaching and discussion may continue till about eleven o'clock. Meanwhile the women and boys are bringing in the single meal. Each one is given a plate, as he sits upon the floor, and on it are heaped rice and curries of different sorts, aud then sweetmeats and fruit. All this must be finished before the hour of noon, for to eat after the shadow has moved beyond the dial-plate's centre is a breach of the sixth precept. There will be no more solid

[1] *Buddhism*, p. 247. Home University Library.

Dagaba at Yatagala Temple, Galle.

food after this till to-morrow's breakfast. Now all is cleared away and baskets of betel-leaves and areca-nut and condiments are brought for the customary chew so dear to the Sinhalese. Meanwhile an elder delivers a short speech on behalf of the rest, returning thanks to those who have supplied the food and maintenance this day, and waited on us so carefully, for we are this day as beggars, and dependent on other's help, even for a glass of water. All must be given. After this comes the slack hour of the day. Some take a turn up and down the hall or corridor, others peacefully ruminate or snatch forty winks, nature and age compelling. Then, as the afternoon draws on, someone will read aloud an article on Ḍhāmma, or a passage from the sacred books, or discuss with the rest some point of difficulty. And so through the long afternoon till tea is served, tea without milk, for milk is animal food, or coriander water. So to our reading and thinking or discussion again, while some few meditate, and "so fleet the time as in the golden age".

Now it is drawing towards sunset, and, as the sun drops behind the trees, we are again to gather at the temple for the evening offerings of flowers, and to renew our morning's vows. Sometimes it is customary to visit a neighbouring temple, if not too far away, and swell the crowd already gathering there. So off we go, each one carrying a lighted candle in his hand, and, as the long procession winds along the village path, lighting up the trees with flickering points of fire, at intervals we raise the cry of "*Sāhḍu*! *Sāhḍu*! *Buḍḍha-parihāra*!" "Glory! Glory! a Buḍḍha-procession!" The whole temple is lit up with tiny lamps, oil-bowls with floating wicks, outlining the dome of the *dāgaba*, while paper lanterns cast a subdued glow upon the walls and trees. Circling thrice clockwise round the *sṭūpa*, we finally fix our candles on the cornice, and await the monk who will administer once more the eightfold vow, after which the "fivefold" devotees in relays take their vows as in the morning; such are the labours of the day. So numerous are those requiring the help of the monks, that the youthful novices take their place, and their shrill voices ring out in the still air, followed by the bass rumble of the men, and women's high-pitched tones. After once more offering flowers and countless sticks of incense, till the whole court and shrine-room smoke again, we gather in a body and sit cross-legged while the aged high priest comes forth to give us a special address on this solemn occasion. He unfolds the course of life leading to the Noble Eightfold Path, and points out how the keeping of these vows now will be to us as stepping-stones across *samsāra's* stream, on the other side of which is the *amaṭapaḍaṁ*, the immortal state of *Nibbāna*.

It is a beautiful scene that meets the eye. The ancient trees, hung with coloured lamps, the soft outline of the dome thrown against the velvet blackness of the star-spangled sky, the wreathing incense-smoke, the flickering candles, the hushed silence of the pauses in the monk's address, and, now and again, a quick patter of bo-leaves overhead, as a breeze arises and dies away again, the white-robed crowd covering the sandy court; while on the ear falls the ceaseless trill of crickets from all sides—all makes an impression of peace and beauty that will never fade from the memory.

Leaving the illuminated temple-grounds, we return to our preaching-hall, and prepare for the third act of our drama, the passing of the night in listening to *Bana*, or preaching of the Law. The lamps have been lit, and one is placed on the preacher's table, where he will sit till sunrise, expounding the Law. Towards eight o'clock the monk who has been selected to preach, generally a scholar of some attainments, enters the hall and takes his seat. The "musicians" now enter to do their service to the Buḍḍha-Ḍhamma-Saṅgha, and commence a terrific salvo of tom-toms and ear-splitting pipes. To stand this needs all our stock of *vairāgya*, indifference. After this "voluntary," the audience, who have been silently gathering, prepare themselves for a full night's exposition of the Law. The monk, after a preliminary clearing of his throat, commences his adoration to the Buḍḍha, in high-toned nasal Pāli verse, then gives out his text, "*Evam me sutaṁ*," "thus have I heard," the commencement of a section of the canon. At the preacher's right hand, seated on the floor, is an elder who acts as "parish-clerk," responding to each pause of the preacher with "*Ehe, svāmi!*" "'Tis so, your reverence!"—and it is to this temporary official that the monk's remarks are really addressed. It sometimes happens that, as it draws towards the still small hours of the morning, this good man is caught nodding, and is reprimanded for his negligence.

And now the preacher is fully launched upon his discourse. A pariah dog strolls in, sniffs round the room and sits calmly in the midst, assiduously attending to his skin. Now and again, a child's shrill voice arises, and his mother takes him out. The audience rise and go in and out at will, for a large part only intend "keeping up" till midnight, when the first discourse will end. Those who have taken the eightfold vow will carry on till dawn. The preacher's theme is the familiar one of the evolutionary scheme of the universe, as set forth by the Buḍḍha. It is the *Paṭiccasamuppādo*, the origination of cause from cause, the fundamentals of Buḍḍhist doctrine. He tells how from ignorance, *avijjā* (unconsciousness rather), arise aggregations, *saṅkhārā*, the first vibrations in *ākāsa*; from *saṅkhārā* comes consciousness of externals, *viññāna*; and from this is formed *nāmarūpa*, name and form, subject and object, and this develops the six centres of sense, *salāyaṭanāni*; then comes contact with externals, *phasso*, resulting in sensation, *veḍanā*. Sensation causes desire for more violent sensation, *ṭanhā*, longing; thus arises *upāḍāna*, clinging to existence, and this gives *bhava*, conception in the womb. Then follows *jāṭi*, birth into the outer world, with all its attendant sorrows, *ḍukkha*, evil, mental pain caused by the impermanence of all things, *jarāmaraṇam*, decay and death, *sokaparideva-ḍukkha-domanassa-upāyāsā*, lamentation, woe, grief and despair. And so the wheel rolls on.

One by one, the audience begin to nod. Here and there a lamp has flickered out. It is nearly midnight, for our discourse has taken long expounding. Outside, utter silence reigns. A few of the faithful remain alert and attentive, but many have succumbed and lie in blissful slumbers, lulled to rest. At one the sermon closes and attendants bring water or coffee, to rouse the attention of the devotees, and nerve them for a second spell of preaching.

The new preacher has a hard task, for he has to wrestle with the powers of sleep, and by hook or by crook so fix the attention of his hearers that they may watch with him until the dawn. His text is the story of the Great Decease, the passing of the Buḍḍha, from *Mahāparinibbānaṁ Suttam*, and he teaches how, though the Buḍḍha has passed away, He has left us the Dhamma as our Comforter, and the promise of a Great One to come. Then quoting the sonorous Pāli, he describes the kindly words of the great Teacher, His last utterance to His beloved disciple Ānanḍa. One passage will suffice for our quotation.

Then said the Blessed One to Saint Ānanda, sitting by his side: "Hush! Ānanda! Let not your heart be troubled. Weep not. Have I not ere now told you that all dear, delightful things have the nature of differentiation, separation, otherness (*nānābhāvo, vinābhāvo, anattābhāvo*)? How can it be then, Ānanda, that what is born, brought forth and composite, of nature to dissolve, can fail to be dissolved? It cannot be. Long, indeed, Ānanda, hast thou waited on Taṭhagaṭo with kindly acts, pleasant and sweet, invariable, unstinted; long hast thou waited on me with kindly words, pleasant and sweet, invariable, unstinted: long hast thou served me with loving thoughts, pleasant and sweet, invariably kind, immeasurable. Right well hast thou done, Ānanda. Persevere with earnestness, and thou shalt attain to utter purity!"[1]

This sermon has lasted some four or five hours. The lamps are fading in the strengthening light of dawn. The chill clean-scented air that marks the coming day blows in through the open windows. An elder rises and with folded palms offers to the preacher a cloth or shawl, or coverlet for rainy nights, as a small return for his careful exposition of the Law, and as a means, too, of acquiring merit. The audience now prostrate themselves, as a mark of reverence to the Order, as the monk leaves the preaching-hall. The sluggards awake, and we all go out to bathe face, hands and feet, and brace ourselves for the completion of our long spell of duties, "lowering the lodge" from the state of eightfold-precept-devotees to that of fivefold-precept-laymen. This done, once more we gather round the *dāgaba*, whose sandy court one of us has already swept before the dawn; once more the aged

[1] MPS. § 14.

high-priest blesses us, this time with the fivefold precept, and for the last time we offer flowers to the relics, the Buḍḍha-image and the tree. Yet one more thing remains, the mutual bestowal, one on another, of the fruits of merit gained by the day's devotion. "Brother! may you share in the merit I have acquired, by taking *Sīla*, by offering flowers, by listening to the Ḍhamma, by meditation and by perseverance." "Brother! I thank you and accept."

"What means all this idolatrous ceremony?" the ignorant may ask. "This is not Buḍḍhism!"

"Pure Devotion," we make reply. "Love for the Brother of mankind, whose strong presence, like the subtle fragrance of a long-closed jar of scent, now opened, suffuses the world, after so many hundred years, a presence that still may help in need 'whosoever thirsteth,' '*yo koci sikkhākāmo hoti,*' though He has for ever passed away." "Brothers! [His dying words] I leave you the Ḍhamma. In it shall I live with you for ever!"

Enough! This day has marked another milestone on our long pilgrimage, and it may be that here and there, by one or two, the Path is nearly reached and knowledge has come in the twinkling of an eye; just as when, after long pondering on some deep problem, hard, profound, not to be solved by mere intellect, suddenly, the changing views of the kaleidoscopic brain crystallise into one-pointedness, and the long-sought clue is found, and the kernel of the matter is displayed; so now in a flash comes *vipassanā*, insight, the goal is nearly won, and all life henceforth takes on a meaning that before was shrouded from our eyes.

Bhikkhus at breakfast in the Olcott Hall, Mahinda College, Galle.

OLCOTT DAY AT GALLE

THE memory of Colonel Olcott is still green in Ceylon. Since his landing at Galle more than thirty-three years ago, along with H.P.B. (on Wesak Day, the day most sacred to the Buḍḍhists) down to the present time, his name has been one to conjure with. His many campaigns in the island on behalf of the Sinhalese Buḍḍhists and the education of their children, the vast crowds which he had the power to draw, and his unsparing labours for "my people," his dignified person and his reverend flowing beard, are still vividly remembered.

Here at Galle we keep holiday on February 17th, the anniversary of his passing away, and in his memory the *bhikkhus* are fed, sermons are preached and flowers offered at the temples. We are up at sunrise this morning, and gather large baskets of flowers, which we carry to the temple, and, after taking the vows of the five precepts, we lay the flowers on the stone slabs of *dāgaba* and image-house, fix our minds on his meritorious acts and ask the blessings of the *Ḍevas* on his name and work.

2

All ṇight long the women-folk have been busy making curry-stuffs, boiling rice, grating cocoanut, chattering and thoroughly enjoying themselves, as they do on these occasions, for it is no light task to entertain some seventy *bhikkhus*, as we mean to do before noon to-day. Some have been busy making coloured paper lamps, an art in which the Sinhalese are adepts, and this evening the whole place will glow like fairyland. Others have cleared the great hall of its desks and benches; mats are spread and the dhoby is hanging white cloth all round and placing cushions up and down and across. The boys are gathering bunches of flowers, dark blue and yellow and orange, to set above the portraits of "the Benefactors," which hang along the top end of the great Olcott Hall.

The flagstaff is gaily decorated with the College and Buḍḍhist flags, the latter of which the Colonel himself introduced into Ceylon. It represents the actual colours of the Lord Buḍḍha's *aura*, His six colours being *nīlo, pīto, lohito, odāto, mañjettho, pabhassaro;* that is, dark blue, yellow, crimson, white, orange, and "radiant". No banner looks so beautiful in decorations as this.

Now it is ten o'clock, and it is time to fill the bowls. Armed with a huge spoon we lead the way and put one spoonful into each of the earthen begging-bowls which have already been brought from the monastery where the monks are gathering. All who wish to acquire merit follow suit until the bowls are nearly full. "A meal for three grown men," you may say. But remember that the attendant boys eat what is left. Besides, the more in the bowl the more room for merit-winners. This is called "paving the way to Nibbāna"; every little helps, so add your contribution, but with goodwill, or it will have no effect.

By half past ten all is ready, and a party goes off to the temple to escort the *bhikkhus* in procession with tom-tom and wail of pipes. Meanwhile we set large tubs of water at the door to wash the *bhikkhus'* feet when they arrive. The crowd gathers round the doors, and groups of indescribable beggars spring up as if by magic. They are marshalled by their leader, and even a beggar-king seems to be a man of no mean authority.

Already in the distance the beat of the tom-toms is to be heard and the shrill "skirl of the bagpipes," heralding the approach of the *parihāra* (procession), and the gong begins to boom a welcome. Through the trees below, the yellow robes are shining, and a long line of *bhikkhus* appears walking slowly under the white canopy supported by the boys. The cloth is not quite long enough to cover all of them, and the remainder walk under the umbrellas which every one, monks included, carries in Ceylon. The procession halts at the door while the feet of the *bhikkhus* are washed and wiped, the drums beating the while, and the crowd raising cries of "*sāḍhu* ! *sāḍhu* !" till all are attended to, and have taken their seats round three sides of the hall. In the corner next to the High Priest is set a sort of conical tripod shrine which contains the sacred relics, and in which also an offering of rice and a cup of water are enshrined. This is the offering to the BUḌḌHA; for, although He has passed for ever from our ken, yet gifts to Him, "acts done to the Ṭathāgaṭa," said the sage Nagasena,[1] "notwithstanding His having passed away and not accepting them, are nevertheless of value and bear fruit".

Now the audience gathers in the hollow of the square formed by the *bhikkhus,* and kneeling prepares to take the five precepts, following the lead of the High Priest who intones them. He is an aged, venerable monk, and a much respected friend of the Colonel. Next is repeated the formula of offering the feast in the customary Pāli stanzas, beginning: *Imaṁ bhikkhaṁ saparikkhārā* .... "This food with requisites (we offer)." The food has previously been arranged in front upon the floor and is covered with a white cloth. This cloth is now removed and the bowls are handed round, each doing his best to heap them with good things, "food hard and soft," according to ancient custom, mutton, fish, (for *bhikkhus* are no vegetarians, eating whatever is given), rice, soup, vegetables, curries of all sorts, pickles, a wonderful compound. As this is a special feast, a separate

[1] *Milinda Panha*, 4, 11, 11.

second course is served of sweets, and then *dhikiri*, curds, and *jaggeri*, a sort of molasses, and, when this is done, a basket of chewing necessaries, betel, areca-nut, *chunam* and various spices, together with huge brass spittoons, and a present of a piece of cloth is offered to each *bhikkhu*. Meanwhile the attendants are clearing away, and the monks are ruminating on the vanity of transitory things in general and of food in particular. When the space in the middle has been swept and cleared, mats are spread and we all sit down to receive the thanks of the monks and listen to a sermon about Colonel Olcott and his good deeds and of the merits of *dāna*, charity.

First of all the monks invoke the Blessed Name and then begin to chant the sonorous Pāli of the *Sutta Pitaka*: "Evaṁ me sutaṁ ... Ekaṁ samayaṁ Bhagavā Sāvatthiyaṁ viharati Jetavane Anāthapindikassa ārāme," and so on through the whole passage enjoining the duty of alms-giving; this they do in unison, the vibrations of the nasals and sounding vowels having an indescribable effect which thrills one through and through, and is like taking a shock from a galvanic battery.

Next the selected preacher begins his sermon, which lasts about ten minutes, and, like all sermons of Buḍḍhist monks in Ceylon, is addressed to a single person who sits close to the preacher, and at the close of each sentence exclaims: *Ehe swāmi*, "It is so, Lord!"

At the end of the sermon an interesting little ceremony takes place, as is usual when a *dāni* or alms-giving is given in memory of a dead person. Sitting on the ground in front of the assembly, the chief alms-giver, with another, slowly pours water from a jug into a bowl set upon a dish, until the bowl overflows; meanwhile the monks all chant in unison, led by the person who is thus transferring the merit of the alms to the dead, the following Pāli stanzas from the *Tiro-Kudda Suttaṁ*:

Idan vo ñātinan hotu
sukhitā hontu ñātayo
te ca tattha samāgantvā
nāti-peta samāgatā

May this merit be for the comfort
And bliss of relatives (ḍeceased).
The ghosts of relatives assembling gather
There (where alms are given).

This three times over. Then is added:

Yathā vārivahā purā
Paripurenti sāgaran
Evameva ito diunam
Petānam upakappati

As swollen rivers fill the sea,
What's given from this world of ours
Does profit to the world of ghosts.

After this the monks depart.

The evening brings illuminations, and *bana* (preaching) begins at nine o'clock and lasts till midnight. The subject is 'The True Friend,' an appropriate title. I have tried to describe this part of the ceremony in

Bhikkhus leaving the Olcott Hall.

the article previous to this, where much the same thing takes place; but, this not being a *uposatha* (sabbath) day, the sermon does not last till the dawn, as in the former case.

THE STORY OF THE WEAVER'S DAUGHTER[1]

ONCE upon a time, those folk who dwelt at Ālavi, after the Master had come to Ālavi, invited Him to take a meal and made their offerings. After returning thanks at the conclusion of the repast, the Master said: "Inconstant is the life of man, certain is death; it needs must be that I should die; death is the end of life for me; in truth life is uncertain, certain is death! Thus should ye meditate on death with concentrated mind. Those folk who have not meditated thus on death are panic-stricken when death cometh, and make their end with wailing, just like a man who seeth a snake with horror and affright. But those who on death have meditated fear not at all, just like a man who from afar beholds a snake and, seizing a

[1] *Pesakavadhitaya Vatthum.* This beautiful and typically Buddhist story of the little maid, who loved the Lord and was true till death, is contained in the Pāli Commentary on the *Dhammapada* [Vol. 3, *Pali Text Society's* Edition]. The greater part of this commentary is made up of illustrative stories. "The whole work," says Professor Norman, "constitutes a species of *Acta Sanctorum*, enforcing by multitudinous concrete examples the theory of *karma* laid down in the fundamental text with which the *Dhammapada* opens: *Manopubbangamā dhammā.*" All states are results of thought.

stick, rids himself of it.[1] Therefore should ye practise the meditation on death."

Now, when they heard this teaching of the Law, the other folk turned to their affairs (and straightway forgot it all), but a little maid of sixteen years said to herself: "O wonderful indeed is the talk of Buḍḍhas! 'Tis fitting that I should practise this meditation on death." So day and night she practised it for full three years.

Now one day the Master, at the early dawn of day, was looking over all the world, and, seeing that the little maid had come within the network (*aura*) of His thought, (*ñānajālassa anto paviṭṭhaṁ disvā*) He said: "Now how is this?" And looking closely at the thing He said: "This little maid, for full three years since first she heard my teaching, has practised the meditation on Death. Now, therefore, will I go thither and put to her four questions, and, if she answers them, I shall praise her on those four points and say to her this verse:

> Blind is the world; and few there be that see:
> Just as a bird that 'scapes the fowler's toils,
> So few there be that find the way to heaven.

And when I have pronounced the verse she will stand established in the First Path's Fruits, and all the crowd shall gain profit by her illustration of my preaching."

[1] This does not mean *kills* it, but removes it in the orthodox fashion (*ahimsena*), as seen in the East, of removing snakes.

With this intent He left the Jetavana with a following of five hundred monks, and thereafter reached the Aggālava monastery.

The folk who dwelt at Ālavi, on hearing that the Master was come, went to the monastery and offered Him a meal. And she, too, that little maid, on hearing that the Master was arrived, with joy exclaimed: "They say that my Father, my Lord, my Teacher, whose face shines like the moon when it is full, even the great Gauṭama the Buḍḍha, hath arrived! 'Tis full three years since the Master, who shines like gold, was seen by me! And now shall I win the sight of His all-golden body, and hear His honey-sweet most excellent teaching of the Law!"

But her father, on going to the shed, said: "Dear child, the cloth I have begun to weave is bespoke by another customer: there is yet a span of it unwoven. I must finish it to-day, so quickly charge the shuttle and fetch it here."

Then she thought to herself: "I am longing to hear the Master's preaching of the Law—and now father says this to me! How can I hear the Law? Well! I must fill the shuttle for father and take it with me."

Then the thought arose in her: "If I do not bring the shuttle, father might strike and kill me; so I will charge the shuttle, take it to him, and then go and hear the Law." So down she sat upon a stool, and charged the shuttle with the flax.

Now the folk of Ālavi had made their offerings to the Master, had taken His bowl and stood waiting for Him to render thanks (*anumodanatthāya aṭṭhaṃsu*). The Master thought to Himself: "I have come here some thirty *yojanas*,[1] all for the sake of this daughter of a household, and to-day she cannot get a chance of coming. When she gets her chance and comes, I will return my thanks." So He sat there and was silent. *Now when the Master holds His peace, nor gods nor men dare say a syllable.*

So it happened that she, the little maid, having charged the shuttle, put it in her basket, and on her way home she reached the outskirts of the gathering; and as she went she cast a shy glance upon the Master. And the Master also lifted up His head and glanced at *her*. And she knew by the manner of His glance: "The Master sits in such a great gathering as this, and looks at *me*, and is waiting for my coming! Into His very presence He waits for *me* to come!"

So she laid aside her basket with the shuttle and drew near the Master.

Now, why did the Master look at her? it may be said. 'Twas thus He thought: "This little maid, on going hence, will die in unbelief, and go on an uncertain devious path. But if she come to me, upon her coming she will win the fruits of the First[2] Holy Path (*Sotāpattiphalaṁ*), and, treading a path

[1] A *yojana* is about 12 miles.
[2] *Buḍḍhi* will be awakened in her by the Master's word.

of certainty, will be reborn in the Heaven of Delight."

And on that very day, 'tis said, her fate was sealed (*maraṇato mutti nāma n'atthi*). There was no means of escape. So she drew near the Master by intuition of His glance, and entering within the aura of the six-hued rays that shone forth from Him,[1] she bowed herself before Him and stood aside; and there she stood after saluting the Master, who sat in silence amid that vast assemblage. Then said the Master:

"Child, whence comest thou?"

"Lord, I know not whence I come," was the reply.

"Whither goest thou?"

"I know not, Lord."

"Thou knowest not?"

"I know, Lord."

"Knowest thou?"

"I know not, Lord!"

So thus the Master asked four questions. And the people were annoyed and cried: "See here! Yon weaver's maid is talking to the all-enlightened One just as she pleases (*icchiticchitaṁ katheti*). When asked: 'Whence comest thou?' pray, why did not she reply: 'I come from home, from the weaver's shed'? And when He asked: 'Whither goest thou?' she should have made reply: 'To the weaver's shed I go'!"

Then the Master silenced the crowd and said: "Child when I asked: 'Whence comest thou?' why

[1] Chabbaṇṇānam ramsinau antaraṁ pavisitvā.

didst thou make reply 'Lord, I know not whence I come?'"

"Lord, thou knowest whence I come—from the weaver's shed. But when thou askedst: 'Whence comest thou?' 'twas meant, methinks: '*Coming whence art thou here reborn?*' And I know not, Lord, whence coming I am here reborn."

Then said the Master: "Well said! well said, indeed! Child, thou hast answered the question that I put."

And thus He praised the little maid and said again: "And when I asked thee: 'Whither wilt thou go?' why didst thou say: 'I know not, Lord'?"

"Lord," she replied, "thou knowest surely that I had taken the shuttle in my basket and was going to the weaver's shed; but Thy meaning really is, methinks: '*Whither going wilt thou be reborn?*' and I know not where I shall be reborn when I have fallen hence (*cutā ito*)."

Then said the Master; "Truly, indeed, hast thou answered the question put by me." And again He praised her, and asked once more; "And when I said 'Thou knowest not?' why didst thou say 'I know'?"

"Lord, *I know that I must die*, and that is why I spoke thus."

"And when I asked thee 'Knowest thou?' why didst thou reply 'I know *not*'?"

"Lord, I know that I must die—*but the hour of my death I know not*; whether it shall be at night, or in the day, or when the sun is high, or at such and such a time, I know not; and that is why I thus replied."

Then said the Master: "Thou hast replied to my question," and a fourth time He praised her, and then turning to the crowd He said: "So many of you know not what she meant. So you are angry with her merely for that. Ah! blind indeed are they who have not wisdom's eye: but they have eyes who wisdom have." And then He spake this verse:

Blind is the world; and few there be that see.
Just as a bird, that 'scapes the fowler's toils,
So few there be that find the way to heaven.

Now at the end of His discourse, the little maid was established in the Fruits of the First Initiation, and the teaching was of great benefit to the multitude.

So the little maid took her basket and shuttle and went away to her father's. Now he had fallen asleep while seated at his work, and as she set down the basket and shuttle, by some mischance it struck the beam end of the loom, and down it fell with a clatter. Up started the father from his sleep, resumed his task and pulled to the loom, and the end of it smote the little maid upon the breast, and down she fell and died upon the spot. And when her father saw her fallen dead, her body soaked with blood, great grief arose in him and he exclaimed: "None other than the Master can end my sorrow now!"

So with lamentation he drew near the Master and told Him all, saying: "Lord! end thou my sorrow!"

And then the Master comforted him, saying : "Sorrow not, for in the endless revolution of this world[1] thou hast indeed shed far more tears than would suffice to fill the oceans four." And with these words He expounded unto him the round of birth that has no rest. And, when the man's sorrow had abated somewhat, he begged the Master for the robes, and received the ordination of the less and greater rank,[2] and in due time he reached the state of Arhaṭ, the Saint.

---

[1] *Samsāra.*

[2] *Pabbajjupasampadā*—as Christians might say "the orders of deacon and priest"

AN ORDINATION OF BUḌḌHIST MONKS

At the edge of the lake at Kandy, hidden away among the trees, there stands an ancient monastery, secluded and unknown to many of the visitors who throng the courts of the Temple of the Tooth on the other side. It is the Malwatte Vihāra (Flower Garden Retreat), the residence of the head of the Buḍḍhist Order in Ceylon, the Mahānāyaka Thero, or Lord High Abbot of the Siam Sect of monks. Here is performed the ceremony of admission to the ranks of the Brethren of the Yellow Robe. An ordination may take place anywhere, provided that it is conferred by a chapter of ten elders, *thera's*, or monks of ten years' standing; but the seal of importance is added by the ceremony taking place at this Kandy head-*vihāra*, and this is usually done on Wesak Day, the great Buḍḍhist festival, the full moon day of the month of May.

To be ordained a monk is a solemn step, and to be ordained upon this day of days, when the heart of every Buḍḍhist is fixed upon the Birth, the Illumination, the Preaching of the Good Law, and the Parinibbāna or final passing away of the Teacher of Gods and men, and here in this place, where for centuries the succession apostolic has been preserved,

The Temple of the Tooth, Kandy.

confers a spiritual touch and awakens associations that are in their way unique. Youths from distant villages have come up, attended by their relatives and friends, to receive the robes and take the vow of *pabbajjā,* renunciation of the worldly life. A boy may not do this till he is at least eight years of age. At the age of twenty he may receive full ordination (take priest's orders, as Christians would say) or the *upasampadā.* Till then he is called a *samanera* or novice. All alike, whether novices, or elders, are termed *bhikkhus,* begging monks, and form the Saṅgha or Order of the Buḍḍhist "Church". On this day, too, are present many *samanera's,* attended by their tutors, who have come up to Kandy from monasteries throughout the island.

It is the evening of Wesak Day, and all the place is lit with lamps which cast their stars upon the still surface of the lake, and white-robed forms move to and fro. The hollow booming of the big tom-toms reverberates among the huge overhanging trees. A flight of stone steps leads up from the road to the ordination-hall, now crowded with monks and laymen. A solemnity pervades the atmosphere which is not dissipated by the subdued chatter of the numbers squatting at the lower end. As we enter the hall, the first thing that strikes the eye is the great glass-enclosed Buḍḍha, before whose calmly-seated cross-legged form blink numberless little lights, amid the heaped-up offerings of many-coloured flowers, in front of which, facing outwards, is seated the aged High Abbot, the president of this gathering. Next to him, on either side, in order of seniority of ordination, are ranged the elder monks, and down the two sides of the hall are rows of juniors, in yellow robes of various hues, orange and ochre, russet and lemon, for the hue varies according to the process and times of dyeing. At the bottom stand the candidates, along with a gorgeously dressed figure in the Kandyan national dress, a *ratemahātma*, or chief, who is the head *dāyaka* or trustee of the temple, befrilled and padded out in white muslin and linen, his fingers decked with jewelled rings; an imposing figure of a man, in strong contrast to the meek and simply-clad close-shaven monks, an ivory-topped garden of sunflowers. The white-clad laymen squatting on the floor form an appropriate background to this scene.

In thought one is carried back two thousand and five hundred years, and pictures to oneself the first giving of the robes by the Master Himself. "Come, monk! (*ehi bhikkhu*)"—this, and nothing more, marked the admission of Yaso, the eager youth, to the perpetual brotherhood of the sons of the Buḍḍha. In after-times, when applicants were many, He gave permission for the robes to be conferred by a chapter of ten elders, with a view to a time when He should be no longer with them, and this ceremony has been performed unchanged, age after age, until the present day. One receives the impression that these yellow-robed shaven-headed monks, with their typical cast of features, are a rock of conservatism on which the waves of centuries of thought have beaten and been rebuffed, confused and ineffectual. Our western ways, our tongue and thoughts, have passed here as the foot-prints of the seagull on the ocean's wave, as the gusts on a rocky promontory, "tempest-buffeted, citadel-crowned".

A voice calls the gathering to order. Silence falls for a moment, soon broken by the rumble of the sonorous Pāli invocation, which has resounded down the centuries.

Namo Tassa Bhagavato Arahato Sammāsambuḍḍhassa. Glory to Him the blessed Saint, the all-enlightened One.

A youth in layman's garb comes forward. He is decked with jewels and fine clothes, lent him for the occasion by relatives and friends, the trappings of the worldly life which he has donned to enhance the effect of the sacrifice he is about to make, and which he will presently doff in exchange for the beggar's robes. He is led by a monk who has been his spiritual guide (*upajjho*) during his preparation, who has trained him in the Doctrine (*dhammo*) and the discipline.[1]

[1] I have translated the ritual, with a little condensation, from the Pāli text of *Upasampadā-Kammavācā* (ordination chapter) as given by Dickson (Journ: R. A. S. 1873). His version will partly be found in Warren's *Buḍḍhism in Translations*.

Standing before the president he bows low and says:

"Give me leave. Lord, in compassion confer on me the robes. (*Kneeling*) Lord, I beg the robes of thee." (*thrice.*)

He now presents to the Abbot the bundle of yellow robes, which he is to don, saying thrice these words:

"Lord, in compassion take these yellow robes and confer them on me for the ending of all sorrow, for the winning of the Peace."

He holds out his folded palms, on which the old monk replaces the bundle with trembling hands and fastens the band round his neck, repeating the *mantram* forwards and backwards:

Kesā Lomā Nakhā Dantā Taco
Taco Dantā Nakhā Lomā Kesā

This formula sums up the transitory nature of the human form, compounded as it is of

Hair o' the head, hair o' the body, nails, teeth and skin;
Skin, teeth and nails, hair o' the body, hair o' the head.

Then rising he retires with his sponsor and another monk, who disrobe him of his finery of borrowed plumes, and while the process goes on—for he wears a series of gaily coloured suits, one over the other—prompted by them he chants the stanzas as he assumes the mendicant's yellow robes.

Patisankhā yoniso cīvaraṁ patisevāmi
Yāvad eva sītassa patighātāya unhassa patighātāya.

Damsamakasa vātātapa sirimsapasamphassānaṁ
patighātāya
Yāvad eva hirikopīna paticchādanatthaṁ.

Thoughtful and wise I don the robe
To guard me from the heat and cold,
From flies and gnats, from wind and sun,
From snake-bite, and to hide my shame.

From bare necessity, not for luxury, he puts on the robes, which, under the old dispensation, were made of rags picked from the dust-heap (see the sermon at the end). *Bhikkhus* of the present day carry umbrellas, fans, wear silken robes sometimes, and sandals; some carry purses and otherwise conform to the changing times.

Now he returns, led by his sponsor, and, again standing before the president, bows and says to his tutor.

"Give me leave. Lord, I bow before thee.
Have patience, lord, with my faults.
May the merits I have won be welcomed by my lord.
'Tis meet to give to me the merits that my lord has won.
'Tis well. 'Tis well, and gladly I receive them.
Give me leave. Out of compassion, Lord.
Give me the Three Refuges and the Precepts Ten.
(*Kneeling*) Lord, I beg the Refuges and Precepts."
(*thrice.*)

The precepts are given and repeated by the candidate in faltering tones, with occasional promptings from the tutor. (To the eight given in "A Buḍḍhist Sabbath"[1] add these two.)

"From the use of high or wide couches or seats —I promise to abstain.

From taking gold or silver—I promise to abstain.

These ten precepts I undertake to keep (*Rising and bowing to his sponsor*).

Give me leave. Lord, I salute thee and accept with thanks." (*As above*)

Such is the ceremony of *pabbajjā*. If duly qualified for the full orders the candidate now retires a moment and returns to make an offering to the Abbot and says: "Give me leave. In compassion, Lord, give me thy aid (*nissāyam*). (*Kneeling*) Lord, I ask thy aid. (*thrice*) Be thou my spiritual guide." (*thrice*)

The President. "'Tis well."

The Candidate. "'Tis fitting. Lord, give me leave. I accept. (*thrice*) From henceforth the elder is my charge (*nissāyo*) and I am his." (*thrice*)

He rises, bows and retires alone to the end of the assembly, where his begging bowl is fastened on his back. The tutor now goes to him and leads him up to the president. Another monk stands up and the two address the *saṅgha* (gathering of monks).

The sponsors (*acting for the assembly*). "Give us leave. (*then to the novice*) Thy name is [*e.g.*] Nāga?"

C. "Give me leave. 'Tis so."

S. "Thy spiritual guide is Tissa the elder?"

[1] *Supra.*

C. "Give me leave. 'Tis so."

S. "*Namo Tassa Bhagavato Arahato Sammāsambuḍḍhassa.*" Glory to Him, the Blessed Saint, the all-enlightened One.

First a spiritual guide is to be obtained. This done, we must inquire about the bowl and robes, thus: "Is this thy bowl?"

C. "'Tis so, Lord."

S. "And this thy upper robe?"

C. "'Tis so, Lord."

S. "And this thy under robe?"

C. "'Tis so."

S. "Go and stand yonder." The candidate retires backwards and stands at the end of the hall. Now one of the sponsors addresses the assembly.

"Listen, reverend brotherhood. This Nāga desires ordination from the reverend Tissa. If it be seasonable to the brotherhood, I will instruct Nāga."

They bow to the Lord Abbot and go down to the candidate and cross-examine him thus:

S. "Hear now, Nāga. 'Tis time to tell the truth and speak of facts. In the midst of the brotherhood of monks, when asked, 'Is it true?' 'tis right to make reply ''Tis true,' or as the case may be. Do not hesitate. Be not distressed in mind. I will ask thee thus:

Hast thou diseases such as these: leprosy, boils, dry leprosy, or phthisis, or epilepsy?"

C. "Nay, Lord."

S. "Art thou a human being, a male, a freeman, debtless, no soldier of the king? Hast thou thy parents' consent? Art thou of full age, and are thy bowl and robes complete?"

C. "Yea, Lord."

S. "What is thy name?"

C. "Lord, my name is Nāga."

S. "What is thy preceptor's name?"

C. "Tissa, the elder, Lord."

The examiners now return to the top end and bow to the Abbot. One of them says, addressing the Order: "Listen, O monks. Nāga desires ordination from the Venerable Tissa. He has been admonished by me. If it be seasonable to the brethren that he should approach, let him be told to approach." (to Nāga) "Come hither."

The candidate comes forward, and, between the two monks, bows and kneels, saying: "O, Lord, I ask the brotherhood (*saṅgha*) for full ordination. May the reverend Order have compassion on me and lift me up!" (*This thrice*). He rises and bows.

The Elder to the Order: "Listen to me, O reverend Order. This Nāga is desirous of ordination from the reverend Tissa." (The same as the above examination.) He turns to the monks and says:

"He is free from the hindrances. His bowl and robes are in order. He asks the ordination from the venerable Tissa."

The Hall of Ordination. Malwatte Vihare, Kandy.

He now thrice "puts the motion" to the chapter of monks, saying: "If any approve of the candidate, let him be silent. If any object, let him speak."

If no objection be made, both bow to the Abbot and announce the decision. "Nāga is ordained under the venerable Tissa. The brotherhood approves. This is their decision (*esa ñatti*). Thus I take your decision."

The ordination is now over and the formula of examination is repeated with each candidate. If there be many, as on this occasion, the proceedings are very long, the patience of the audience is exhausted and the monks find it hard to fix their attention on the words, as they had been enjoined to do. A buzz of conversation arises from the lower end. Then, when all have been duly ordained, an elder rises and exhorts the new monks, who stand before him reverently, as follows, with the time-honoured admonitions.

The Preacher. "Now should the shadow be measured.[1] The exact time must be declared. The portion of the day must be recorded. In conjunction these things are to be told. The four supports (*nissāyā*) of the monk and the four forbidden actions must be told. Food collected in a bowl is the monk's support. Thus fed must ye strive, as long as life shall last. These are the extra allowances:—Food given to the Order as a whole, occasional food, invitation food,

[1] The exact time and date of ordination are to be recorded for future reference in case of dispute, for seniority in the Order depends solely on priority of ordination.

ticket food, fortnightly meals, full-moon feasts, and food of the day after the full moon.

The Candidates. "Even so, Lord."

P. "Robes made of rags are the monk's support. Thus clad must ye strive, as long as life shall last. These are the extra allowances:—Robes of linen, cotton, silk, wool, hemp, or made of all these five.

C. "Even so, Lord."

P. "A seat at the foot of a tree is the monk's support. Thus seated must ye strive, as long as life shall last. These are the extra allowances: A residence, a lean-to, an upstairs building, a walled house or a cave."

C. "Even so, Lord."

P. "Ammonia[1] as medicine is a monk's support. Thus physicked must ye strive as long as life shall last. These are the extra allowances:—Butter, cream, oil, honey and sugar."

C. "Even so, Lord."

The Four Forbidden Actions.

P. "The sexual act must not be practised by a fully-ordained monk, nor any act of bestial nature. The monk that follows this pursuit is no monk, no son of the Sākya clan. Just as a man whose head is severed from the trunk can live no longer, so is a monk who follows this pursuit a monk no longer, no son of the Sākya clan. Thus restrained must ye strive, as long as life shall last."

C. "Even so, Lord."

[1] *Pūtimuttaṁ.*

P. "Things not given to him a fully-ordained monk must not take with thievish intent, were it even a blade of grass. The monk that takes thus thievishly a little coin or half a coin or anything worth as much or more than that, if it be not given, is no longer a monk, no longer a son of the Sākya clan. Just as a withered leaf, once severed from the stalk, hath no longer any part in greenness, even so the monk who takes dishonestly what is not given, is a monk no longer, no longer a son of the Sākya clan. Thus must ye refrain, as long as life shall last."

C. "Even so, Lord."

P. "No living thing, were it e'en but an ant, must be deprived of life, with intent to slay (*sancicca*), by a fully-ordained monk. Moreover, if a monk slay a being of human form, even by slaying a foetus in the womb, he is a monk no more, no more a member of the Sākya clan. Just as a rock once split in twain can never be rejoined, so is a monk who takes life, with intent to slay, a monk no more, no more a member of the Sākya clan. From this act ye must refrain as long as life shall last."

C. "Even so, Lord."

P. "No superhuman powers are to be claimed, not even to the extent of saying 'I delight to live in a lonely hut,' by a fully-ordained monk. If a monk deceitfully, for gain, falsely lay claim to superhuman qualities, be it the Trance,[1] the Ecstasy,[2] the Absorption,[3] the Path[4]

[1] *Jhāna.* [2] *Vimokkho.* [3] *Samādhi.* [4] *Maggo.*

or the Path's Fruit[1]—he is a monk no more, no more a member of the Sākya clan. Just as a tall palmyra palm, whose top has been cut off, can never put forth shoots again, so a monk, who deceitfully, for gain, falsely lays claim to superhuman powers, is a monk no more, no more a member of the Sākya clan. These things ye must avoid as long as life shall last."

C. "Even so, Lord."

Our ceremony is now over and the night is far spent. The newly-robed *bhikkhus* go forth with eager hearts, hoping to tread the Path by living in the ancient way; and surely, sooner or later, they shall attain, for not for naught do Buḍḍhas take birth in this world of ignorance; and we, who in thought have been carried back to ages long ago, descend again to the world of *rikshas*, hotels, gas-lamps and railway trains.

---

[1] *Plalaṁ.* Each step of the four Paths has two grades, the Path and the Fruit; the first being the entering on that state and the second the grasping of its blessings.

The Great Dāgaba at Tissamahārāma, S. E. Ceylon.

AT THE FOOT OF A TREE

It is high noon, and not a leaf stirring. Here, where I have sat for long hours through many years, alone, under the shadow of the great wild mango tree, whose girth two long-armed men could not embrace and touch hands, whose branches stretch for many a fathom and lend a generous shade—here in the still heat is utter silence. Even Ttcheekh, the great saw-legged cricket, has trilled himself to sleep, and the ring-dove has forgotten to coo, and preens his plumes on yonder branch. All things save the bees high up aloft are sleeping.

Close by, near that rock in the patch of sunlight, my old friend Nāya, the great cobra, hangs half out of his hole in a deserted ant-hill, a convenient home for him, he thinks, and ready made, and his many exits and re-entrances have worn the hole so smooth that it is like a glove to him, for nothing irritates a snake so much as rough and bristly things. I say "my friend," for we tolerate each other and Nāya does not spread his hood at me, because I never move and startle him; he tolerates me, and I do not take liberties with him nor pull his tail when he is half in his hole and quite defenceless. Nāya is enjoying the sun, and he comes out when it is high and basks silently there. Presently he will emerge, inch by inch, to his full length of seven feet, and glide slowly round the radius of a few yards, licking up the ants with lightning tongue, calm, gentle and lonely. Who can say how long he has lived there, venerated by the villagers as a sage? Even I have known him there ten years. Still, with bright unwinking eyes, he seems to ponder on the secret of things, emblem of eternity and unfathomable wisdom.

Life here is seemingly at a standstill, yet beating at full pressure if we look closer and within. Silently and swiftly along that branch the red ants are running to and fro. There is method in their going, for they stop at every inch and greet the ones they meet, rub feelers and pass along some mystic message, give some pass-word of grave import. Doubtless their part in the great scheme is as important as mine. "And do thou," says Marcus Aurelius, of whom I love to think as the third great Buḍḍhist Emperor, "and do thou frequently consider the connection of all things in the universe and their relation one to the other. For in a manner all things are implicated with one another, and all in this way are friendly to one another, by virtue of mutual conspiration and the unity of substance." "Look inward, thou art Buḍḍha," says the eastern Sage; and "Look inward," says Marcus, echoing the wisdom of the East, "for within is the fountain of good, and it will ever bubble up, if only thou wilt dig." And here, in Nature's lap, we may dig and find,

> Annihilating all that's made
> To a green thought in a green shade.

A sudden flicker of brown and white, a swirl of activity in this place of peace, and across my feet skips *lena* the squirrel, with his stripes of orange and black, chasing his tail, restless and active for sheer joy of living, his bright beady eyes on the alert, and ears pricked up. Suddenly he is aware that I am not a rock after all, nor yet a withered branch, and tries to reassure himself, bounding sideways off and halting doubtfully. Now with a spring of his great muscular thighs he is off and up the tree, and already at the top. Then in contrast, deliberate and slow, hither crawls Bill, the three foot *talagoya,* or minor iguana, quietly browsing on insects, and dragging his uncouth length along with waddling gait. (I call him Bill, from recollections of Bill the lizard, in *Alice in Wonderland.*) How the ants must dread his approach! And yet they are gone and are down his throat before they have time to fear, for he makes short work of six or eight at each swift flicker of that long purple tongue, without seeming to look at his prey. Bill lends a prehistoric touch to the whole scene, with his clumsiness, and legs joined at strange angles to his body. Slow and ungainly though he seem, stir but an inch and he will be off like a shot, resembling nothing so much as an old out-of-date paddle-wheel steamer, going overland with the speed of a motor-car.

Yonder again, shyly capering behind the tree-boles, comes a white-whiskered long-tailed brother, *wandara*, curiously examining this intruder on his privacy, and yet another and another, peeping out behind the trees; then off they go, their purpose forgotten, even before it took birth in the flickering brain.

"*Rukkhamule*—at the root of a tree," said the Buḍḍha, "meditating, with body erect and mind intent, here shalt thou attain the Truth"; and it may well be that the great vegetable peace of a mighty ancient tree, and its slow-vibrating life, produces peace in the bodily vehicles. The One Life is dreaming in the vegetable world and aware, but it is a life of its own, and we mortals cannot see it nor feel it until we are ourselves as still and harmless as the trees, our wholesome one-legged brothers, and tuned down to their note.

This aged tree, the oldest of the country rornd, has been long my friend, and in sympathy I have bathed in his aura many a day and felt his kindliness. In this utter silence he seems to be conscious of me and I of him. Slowly the hours creep on, and time has nearly stood still. The moments draw to an intense point of vibration and suddenly they seem to pause. *Manodvāram vivarati*—slowly the doors of consciousness swing back, and—*fallor an?*—do I dream, or what is yon gracious towering form that swells out from the body of the tree, huge and benign, a *rukkha* ḍeva, tree-deity indeed? Slowly the upper part takes the human shape—a misty radiance below and above—a majestic human head with triple tiara crowned; seemingly aware and yet not noticing, the great profile stares out into vacancy—a mighty kindly presence, spreading peace around, seen in the stillness, unseen and unrevealed in the human noise and stir. I bethink me of that carving, on the famous *sṭūpa,* of the Lord Buḍḍha preaching to the eager-eyed divinities, leaning forward with folded palms out of the sacred bo-tree. Yes, it is no fairy-tale: the tree-gods are still there and waiting for Him who is to come. What sort of consciousness is theirs? Surely their way is peace, and their path is the path of *alma mater, bhūmi devī,* mother nature; and to live according to nature, as the ancients said, is to be attuned with all that lives.

"And I go through the things," says Marcus, "which happen according to nature until I shall fall and rest, breathing out my breath into that element out of which I daily draw it in, and falling upon that earth out of which my father collected the seed, and my mother the blood, and my nurse the milk; out of which during so many years I have been supplied with food and drink; which bears me when I tread on it and abuse it for so many purposes. Therefore

. . . . pass through this little space of time conformably to nature, and end thy journey in content, just as an olive falls off when it is ripe, blessing nature who produced it, and thanking the tree on which it grew."

The fancy fades, and I am again alone under the great tree. A slight shiver passes over the upper boughs. Peace. Surely this is the meaning of "the life according to nature," *dhammena jivitum*—to live according to Law in harmony. And what nobler prayer could mortal offer to the Gods than that of Socrates the sage, who said, while seated beneath the fair plane tree in the *Phædrus*:

"Beloved Pan, and all ye other gods who here abide, grant me to be beautiful in the inner man, and all I have of outer things to be at peace with those within. May I count the wise man only rich. And may my store of gold be such as none but the good can bear."

Such are my musings "at the foot of a tree," and such my glimpse of the beyond; and though I be unfit to pass through those doors, yet, methinks, I have peeped through the key-hole.

PANIDHANAM

LABHEYYANÇA AHAN TASSA METTEYYASAMA-
GAMAN
METTEYYO NAMA SAMBUDDHO TARETI JANA-
TAN BAHUN.

YADA METTEYYATAM PATTO DHAREYYAM
PITAKATTAYAN
TADAHAN PANNAVA HOMI METTEYYAUPA-
SANTIKE TI.

Buddhaghosasuppatti. Gray, p. 68

ASPIRATION

O MAY IT BE MY LOT TO MEET WITH HIM,
THE LORD METTEYYA! HE, BUDDHA SUPREME,
SHALL LEAD VAST MULTITUDES ACROSS SAM-
SARA'S STREAM.

WHEN I HAVE FOUND METTEYYA, MAY I BE
VERSED IN THE SCRIPTURES THREE, AND
FACE TO FACE
THE LORD OF MERCY THEN IN WISDOM I
SHALL SEE.

F. L. W.

METṬEYYA BODHISAṬṬVA

Evam me sutaṁ. "Thus have I heard": "A new Religion cometh; that of Faith must yield to that of Love, to which He who is to be one day the Lord of Love, Meṭṭeyya, shall point the way."

We must needs believe in the progressive illumination of our race, in a revelation by an all-wise One, gradually given forth to those who are ready for it, and fitted for acceptance by an ever-widening circle of believers. It cannot be that we go round and round as in a closed cage. Yet apparently it is so. How often do we pass the masked door that at last stands open to our pressure! "To him that knocketh" that door is always ajar; yet the world in its blindness needs great spiritual Teachers from time to time, who, like the Initiate in Plato's cave, turn round our eyes from the perishing world, till they be enabled to endure the gazing on the *real* world and the brightest part thereof. But the world moves very slowly, and it is *we* who collectively refuse to be turned to the light, who have our faces persistently turned downwards, absorbed in the petty practices which constitute our life; and our hearts are hardened and our ears are stopped, so that we refuse to listen to the voice of the charmer, charm he never so wisely. Thus even the Lord Buḍḍha was hedged about and limited by force of circumstance, and could not preach His incomparable Dhamma in a land where its basis was unknown—for it was unknown outside the Holy Land of Mother Gangā, the fountain-head of true Religions; so strictly is the greatest power confined by destiny's iron band.

And now, after two thousand and five hundred years, what hope of further progress, stimulated by further teaching? Can it not be said that we are nearer Brotherhood? The world is now one vast parish; its bonds of unity are drawn tighter; and in this age of quick transit, of lightning communication, when we can know in a moment what is passing in the world's remotest corner, all men are knit closer by the ties of friendly intercourse. Again, two or three widespread languages afford a near approach to a universal tongue. Although, on the one hand, this great intimacy means keener rivalry and greater thirst for possessions and self-expansion, so that at times men's passions are at boiling point, yet, on the other hand, there is a greater regard for man as man and brother; there is greater knowledge, greater hope, and a looking round in all directions for one to loose the knot, the tangle which we have reached; a turning of all eyes "to the hills whence cometh our help," a longing for a Teacher of gods and men, once more to tread the earth and walk amongst us in kindly human form. The times are ripe for His coming. The Sibyl, the old ever-young maiden Isis, once more presents us with her ancient books; once more the ambassador of Kings holds his hand beneath his robe, and it is *take* or *leave,* for weal or woe; and the gift he there conceals is that of peace, not war.

This idea of the possibility of a Supreme Teacher, from time to time appearing, is, curiously enough, rejected, or so it seems, by the very people who profess to believe it—the Buḍḍhists and the Christians;—the Christians, talking always of Him that is to come, and at the same time rejecting the idea that such a coming is possible—that He is to come, a real man, a Brother—not dreaming of its possibility both here and now, but relegating it to some time unspeakably distant, when they (who are ready) shall be carried up into some paradise, and *they* only are to be His chosen ones;—and the Buḍḍhists, talking always of Maitri Bodhisat, and hoping that He will take them to Nirvāna, by some unaccountable process of easily gotten illumination, and yet, contrary to the teaching of their own Scriptures, holding that the Path is closed, banish the Blessed-one-to-come to some inaccessible *Tusita Deva-Loka,* where He is supposed to remain for incalculable æons till a *future kalpa;* forgetful that the Lord Buḍḍha, as Bodhisat, took birth for hundreds of lives amongst us, even when we were all animals or less evolved. Little do the Christians reck of the promise that the Comforter should come, and came; and little do the Buḍḍhists dream that, when Gauṭama the Buḍḍha passed away, after watching over us for countless ages, His great successor took the burden of the world upon His shoulders, and bore it, unknown and unthanked, and is still bearing it, and will bear it among us miserable men, and will come again to set the feet of thousands on the Path of Righteousness, that they may run their course and be ready to take the final step with Him in His last appearance on this earth. That time, indeed, may be far off, but we may hasten it by our energetic striving; but many times He needs must come ere then, and the cycle has come round once more, for the star is seen in the East, and the planets point like a dial in the sky. Yet if one asks a Buḍḍhist of to-day, "What of the Bodhisat?" the answer comes, "Oh! He is in Tusita-heaven till next kalpa?" *Till next kalpa*! and meanwhile the hearts of men are aching, and the world awaits the disentangler of the coil.

If we Buḍḍhists would be abreast of modern science, which in words we claim to be by virtue of the Dhamma, we must needs awaken to the thought that this Dhamma, if scientific, must be progressive and evolutionary, that illumination reaches indefinitely onwards. We have to remember that the knowledge which is meant for strong men (as we now claim to be by virtue of the advances of modern science—science which has trained the world in general to familiarity with the natural forces which in the Buḍḍha's time were regarded as miraculous) that this knowledge could not have been revealed to us when we were babes in the infant class of three thousand years ago. We must remember that it is by our own painful progress, step by step, by careful testing of the facts, by sufferings self-imposed by our *kamma*—that it is by these that we have won to higher ground, that it is due to our leaders of humanity who have suffered at the hands of the world (which hates all those who rise above it), suffered martyrdom ever for our sake—to uphold the torch of knowledge above the rushing flood and hand it on in a glorious *lampadéphoria* by relays to the goal—the inheritors of late renown—the Socrates and Jesus, the Hypatias, the Galileos, the Brunos,

> And many more, whose names on earth are dark,
> But whose transmitted effluence cannot die.

It is by these, led by our great Pioneer, the Buḍḍha, that our progress has been made possible; we tread on the bones of the heroes who have died, who went before us and trod a path in the jungle, that a still greater teaching might be given to the world, for which in those dark ages the world in general was not yet ripe.

For there was not opportunity, perhaps, to give out a message which should satisfy all needs. The Christ spoke words of simple morality, the sermon on the

Mount, probably nearly all that we have of the original teaching. The Buḍḍha, on the other hand, did not call men to worship an exalted One, though the natural result was that He is worshipped, in reality, by His followers. Knowledge was His goal. Later expounders of the two creeds which have most stirred the world have filled up what seemed to them deficiencies: thus, as Prof. Edmunds says[1], *Origen attempted to give us the metaphysic neglected by Christ*, and *Asvaghosa added the worship neglected by the Buḍḍha.* We still await the Teacher who shall satisfy us in both. "The Christ-Metteyyo," says he, "is yet to come, who shall make the measurement: *the prophet of the perfect balance between mind and heart*, whom Emerson sighed for, and for whom the ages wait."

Well does Sir Oliver Lodge write[2]: "We need not be afraid of an idea because it has several times striven to make itself appreciated. It is foolish to decline a revelation because it has been more than once offered to humanity. *Every great revelation is likely to have been foreshadowed in more or less imperfect forms, so as to prepare our minds and make ready the way for complete perception hereafter.* It is probable that the human race is quite incompetent to receive a really great idea the first time it is offered. There must be many failures to effect an entrance before the final success, many struggles to overcome

[1] *Buddhist and Christian Gospels*, Vol. I, p. 167.

[2] *Hibbert Journal*, July, 1911, p. 701. (Italics mine.)

natural obstacles and submerge the stony products of human stolidity. Lapse of time for general progress is necessary before anything great can be permanently accomplished, and repeated attempts are necessary: *but the tide of general progress is rising, all the time.*

"So it was with the idea of the Messiah which was abroad in the land, and had been for centuries, before Christ's coming; *and never has He been really recognised by more than a few.* Dare we not say that He is more truly recognised now than in any previous ages in the history of the Church—except perhaps the very earliest? And I doubt if we need make that exception."

And again he writes:[1] "No sudden jump into something supernal, but steady and continued progress." And here he is using almost the very words of the Buddha when He said (*Udāna*, v. 5[2]): "The training is gradual, there is a regular succession of duties, progress is made step by step. *There is no sudden penetration into the Higher Wisdom.*"

What the great teachers of old were compelled, through men's ignorance, to put into the form of a parable is now seen to be a far-reaching knowledge of things superphysical and physical which modern science has not yet reached, with all its patient labour. So that, firstly, we are ready in one sense for a Great Teacher, who shall speak out with knowledge,

[1] p. 712 loc. cit.

[2] *Imasmiṁ dhammavināye anupubbasikkhā anupubbakiriyā anupubbapatipadā n' āyataken' eva aññāpativedho.*

by reason of our greater knowledge. We are clamouring at the gate which opens to a further region, and daily the cry for the keeper of the Keys rings louder in our ears.

And, secondly, *by reason of our greater need.* The struggle for life was never so great, and the lofty heights of pleasure and light, which the more fortunate in life's race have won, are balanced by an ever-deepening gloom among the submerged tenth of our fellow-creatures.

> My son, the world is dark with griefs and graves;
> So dark that men cry out against the heavens.
> Who knows but that the darkness is in man?
> The doors of Night may be the gates of Light.

And, as our need is greater, so are our hearts more ready and expectant: so that, thirdly, *by virtue of our compassion* we are ripe for the coming of Him whose name is Compassion—the Lord Meṭṭeyya. And if such a Teacher is to come, great as He may be, He cannot hew His way alone. Even the Buḍḍha, after He had climbed to that great height of Initiation which we term *Nirvāna,* experienced even here on earth, was for a moment lost in dejection at the very immensity of His discovery, so that He hesitated to teach it to mankind; and yet, for the sake of a few—*Ye keci sikkhākāmā honti*—whosoever thirsted, whose eyes were not wholly dust-concealed—He gave it out, and cast His net, and drew in a fisher's harvest, many thousand souls, long prepared through ages past, and set up a Light which still shines, and once more in these latter days illuminates the world—He whom countless millions call *Devadevo, Sallakatto, Satthà, Dipolokassa*—God of Gods, Great Physician, Teacher, Light of the World—causing ten thousand worlds to shout for joy, having attained to Supreme Enlightenment upon the Bodhi throne, He passed beyond the successive waves of life and death, the long *samsāra* wherein all are plunged.

And strange it is to note that the very home of His Incomparable Dhamma, the India that He loved, is now without His teaching! So said a Christian Bishop, lecturing lately in the West. True enough! but this good man forgot that Christianity, pure and simple, is also quite extinct in the land where first it was announced. Such is the march of destiny. And, after all, this is a reasonable thing, for we cannot expect that the devotees of a religion are born and re-born time after time in the same land where first they learned their Faith. So that we may well think these now deserted lands may some day hear a fresh and later version of that same teaching in a different form.

But to revert to the preparing of the way. I said, He cannot do without our help. That He took birth so many times in the East was due to the fact, no doubt, that *there* was a race prepared by tradition and immemorial custom to welcome Him. He now comes, we think, not to the East alone, but to the world; and since His name is ever *Meṭṭeyya*, Compassionable, it is *we* who must open our hearts to compassion and love of one another, and we only need the will to do it; for, as says Asvaghosa, there is an inherent fundamental *maitri* (mercy) and *karuna* (sympathy) in each being, which is galvanized into life by the presence of a sage or Buḍḍha. And *how* to galvanize this latent feeling into life? The Buḍḍha Himself has told us, by *Mettabhāvanā*, "development of a heart of goodwill towards all living beings"; and the fruits are these, as one of the ancient books records. Says King Milinda:

> Acchariyan, bhante Nāgasena, abbhutan, bhante Nāgasena,
> Sabbapāpanivāranā mettābhāvanā ti.—
> Sabbakusalagunāvahā, mahārājā, mettābhāvanā hitānam-pi
> Ahitānam pi, ye te sattā viññānabaddhā sabbesan
> Mahānisansā mettābhāvanā sanvibhajitabbā ti.—(Mil. Pan. 200.)

> "Strange! passing strange! All evil states of mind
> Are banished by Love's contemplation."
> "Protective of all happy states, O King,
> Is that Love-Practice, *to all living things,*
> *Both good and ill*; of blessing unsurpassed
> To every creature bound in consciousness
> Is that Love-Practice, and unstintingly
> Should it be realised by us, O King!"

"All beautiful things," said Plato long ago, "all beautiful things are hard of attainment." And it is not by sitting still inactive, waiting for a glorious consummation, that we shall help on the evolution of the world—for such we deem to be our task, and to each has fallen by *kamma* some task he can perform—but by all jointly labouring for a common end; thus may we proclaim ever that Incomparable Dhamma.

Bahujanahitāya bahujanasukhāya lokānukampāya
Atthāya hitāya sukhāya devamanussānan.

For the blessing of the many,
For the profit of the world,
For compassion on the world,
For the profit, for the blessing, for the bliss
Of *Devas* and mankind.

So may we, by fellowship and brotherly love, make less thorny the path on earth of our Master and Teacher, who is to be Meṭṭeyya—but who cannot enter our hearts against our will, who cannot even be recognised by those who have not the heart of love—He who is, as Shelley sings,

That *Light*, whose smile kindles the Universe;
That *Beauty*, in which all things work and move
That *Benediction*, which the eclipsing curse
Of birth can quench not; that sustaining *Love*
Which, through the web of being, blindly wove
By man and beast and earth and air and sea,
Burns bright or dim, as each are mirrors of
The *Fire* for which all thirst.

The Vasanṭā Press, Adyar, Madras.